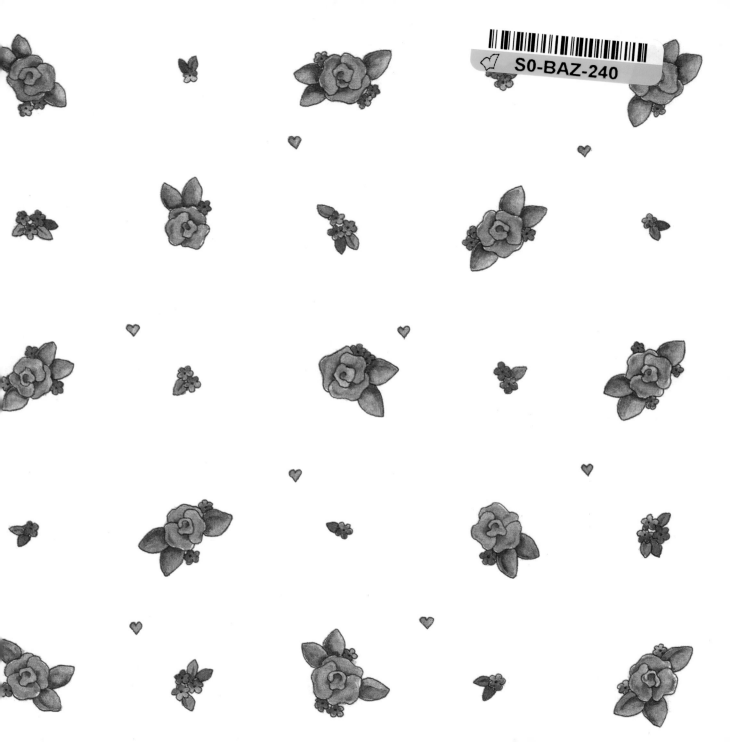

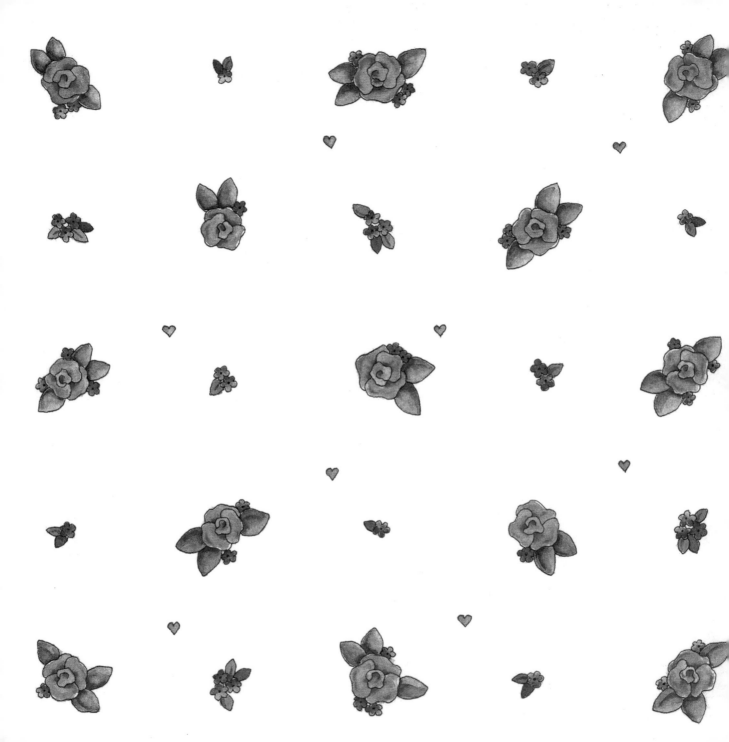

Presented to:

From:

Dedicated to my daughter

Michelle Allen

with love

Love in Every Room

handwritten
to delight & inspire
the heart of every woman
who pursues the
high & holy calling
of
keeper of the home.

by

KARLA DORNACHER

COUNTRYMAN

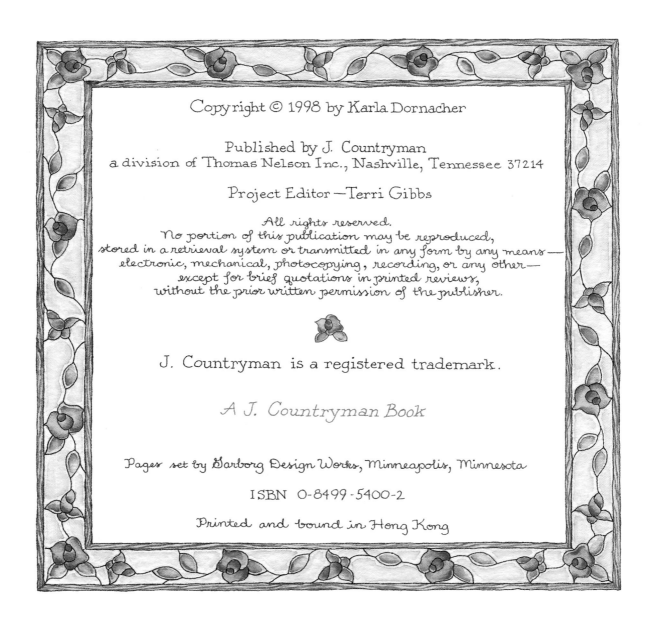

Published by J. Countryman
a division of Thomas Nelson Inc., Nashville, Tennessee 37214

Project Editor—Terri Gibbs

J. Countryman is a registered trademark.

A J. Countryman Book

Pages set by Garborg Design Works, Minneapolis, Minnesota

ISBN 0-8499-5400-2

Printed and bound in Hong Kong

 # Welcome my friend!

Come in, come in and make yourself at home. I'd like to invite you to walk with me through the rooms of a very special house — a house designed to embrace your heart, comfort your soul, challenge your mind, and delight your eye. Together we will pause to capture the beauty of its furnishings, discover some of its hidden treasures, and maybe even be invited to dinner.

Through short stories and illustrations of things that are familiar and common to our daily lives, I hope you will see some of God's truths in a new and personal way.

I'm sure you will find your visit to be refreshing, inspiring, and delightful. So please, come along and enjoy yourself.

Your friend,
Karla ♥

Bless this home as we come and g

bless this home as we enter i

6

less this home as the children grow,

bless this home with love & friends.

7

A
house is a
physical building,
walls that shelter, protect,
and sometimes even divide.
A *home* is the invisible structure,
radiant love
that embraces each member of the family and reaches out
to draw in friends, neighbors, and strangers.

♥

As a woman, God has called you to be
the heart and the keeper of your home.
It is a position of influence and responsibility,
as well as honor and great reward.

♥

This high calling is an expression of God's own heart,
for as you allow His love to fill your life
and spill over to touch the lives of others,
that same love will warm your home
and the hearts of all who enter there.

♥

God in you . . . . the heartbeat of the home.

As for me and my house, we will serve the Lord.

Joshua 24:15

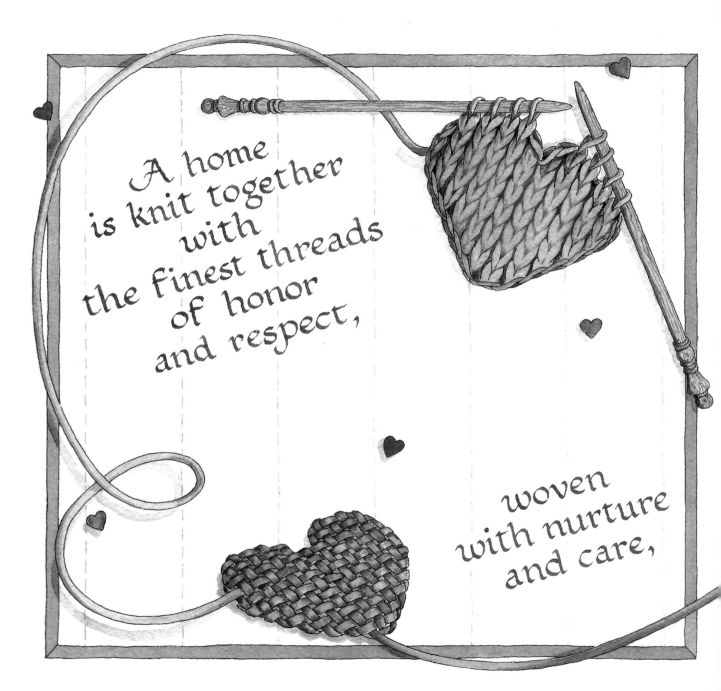

A home
is knit together
with
the finest threads
of honor
and respect,

woven
with nurture
and care,

held securely
in place
by cords
of love

and

11

You stand at the door, hesitant to knock.
You have a list of challenges you're facing as keeper of your home,
but you don't know what to do.

God does not want you to stay outside on the porch
and face your struggles alone.
His welcome mat Welcome is always out and His door unlocked.
He invites you to come in and share your heart with Him.
He has promised to help if you will just ask;
He will care for you as a shepherd cares for the sheep.

Knock and the door of God's love
and blessing will be opened to you.

Enter into His presence for there you will find
refreshment and rest for your soul,
and the light of Christ to guide you through your day.

And what about those who are knocking at your front door?
As the keeper of your home,
you have been called by God to be hospitable.
Take time to put out your welcome mat and open your heart
to those who knock at your door: family, friends,
neighbors, even those you do not know.
Invite them in to share in your life
and the blessings you have been given.

Knock
and
it will be
opened
to you

Matthew 7:7

Welcome

Kick off your shoes,
make yourself at home,
come sit in a comfy chair.

Our lives, our love,
our joy and laughter,
with you, we gladly share.

16

KEEPING A HOME, NURTURING OTHERS, AND FACING LIFE'S DAILY CHALLENGES CAN EASILY LEAVE YOU TIRED, WEARY, AND BURDENED. JESUS IS WAITING TO GIVE YOU REST FOR YOUR SOUL.

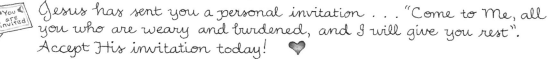

Jesus has sent you a personal invitation . . . "Come to Me, all you who are weary and burdened, and I will give you rest". Accept His invitation today! ♥

On the back of the chair lies a quilt of many colors, a symbol of favor. Let your heavenly Father wrap you in His quilt of love and tenderness so you will know how special you are to Him. You are the apple of His eye!

God wants you to cast your cares upon Him. He will take your cares and cover them over, so you can rest in Him.

The Holy Spirit, represented by the dove, comes to you as your comforter, to speak peace to your heart and to guide you. ♥

The lamp is a reminder that Jesus came to be the Light in your darkness.

As you spend time with Him, you will see the beauty and the majesty of His loving care even in the midst of your circumstances.

Use this quiet time to reflect and meditate on God's Word.

Come, worship at God's footstool, for His Word says that as we humble ourselves before Him, He will lift us up. ♥

17

Fond memories
and
a glowing fire
are kindred friends.

♥

Both delight
the heart
and warm the home.

Like true love, praise is not
based on emotion but on a decision.
Your feelings may say there is nothing to be thankful
for, but by choosing to focus on what is true, good, and
worthy of praise, you can change your thoughts and your attitude.
And when you praise God with your mind,
your heart is soon to follow.

If you are not in the habit of praising God, begin today.
Celebrate all He has done for you and the wonder of who He is.

And remember . . . children learn best from example. The importance of passing on
the habit of praise to your children cannot be overemphasized!

If you need inspiration, read the Word of God, especially the book of Psalms.

God gave you your voice, so why not lift it up to Him in praise?
Don't wait until Sunday... turn on the music and praise Him today!

Worshipping at God's footstool has a way of putting things
on this earth into proper perspective.

From the rising of the sun to it's going down
the Lord's name is to be praised.

Psalm 113:3

Let everything that has breath praise the Lord

Psalm 150:6

Count your blessings name them one by one

Use this space to "count your blessings".
Consider the things we often take for granted,
such as air to breath and water to drink.

You have been invited to a banquet prepared by the Lord Himself!
He wants to set before you foods that are guaranteed
to delight your palette and nourish your soul.
Come, taste and see for yourself just how wonderful and good He is.

This is a "come as you are" dinner. You don't have to dress up.
You don't have to hide your scars, weaknesses, or failures, for He sees you
through the eyes of unconditional love. And to Him you are beautiful.
He wants you to come just as you are to His table of goodness and grace.

Just as He fed the multitudes with the loaves and fishes,
Jesus has promised to supply your needs as well.
Accept His invitation. Take time to sit at His table.
Open your Bible and allow Him to fill your empty plate.
"Chew" the Word thoroughly, meditate on it and think about how it applies
to your life. Then allow it to become part of who you are, nourishing,
refreshing, and energizing your very being.

As you look upon this table let the bread remind you that Jesus is
the Bread of Life, the source of all you need. He has promised to bring you
to a land of milk and honey, a place of spiritual abundance. The
herbs and vinegar are reminders of the variety of flavors —
both sweet and bitter — that God uses to season our days.

When you partake of the Lord's feast, trusting and believing in
His provision for every area of your life, you will be able to lead others,
especially your children, to the table of the King.

Taste and see

Psalm 34:8

that the Lord is good

The fruit of the Spirit is love, joy, peace, patience, kindne

♥ goodness, faithfulness, gentleness and self-control ♥

Fruit·of·the·Spirit Salad

Fill a house with equal & bounteous portions
of Love, Joy, and Peace.

Add to it abundant quantities of Patience.

Sprinkle generously with acts of Kindness
& Goodness.

Stir heartily with boundless Faithfulness,

Cover carefully with Self-Control,

Serve to overflowing with great Gentleness.

A Sweet Treat for Family and Friends

27

Whatever you do, do it heartily,

as to the Lord and not to men.

Colossians 3:23

There's order and there's disorder . . . and there's somewhere in between.
To be a perfectionist in your housekeeping is not only no fun, it's not healthy
for you or your family. On the other hand, neither is being a slob.
There is, however, a certain degree of orderliness and cleanliness
necessary to create a pleasant, comfortable, and safe home.

Most importantly, remember that whatever you do, be it
dishes , laundry , sweeping  or cleaning
do it with your whole heart

to bless . . . not impress!

Determine to let the focus of your housekeeping chores
be to bless the Lord, your family, and your guests.
Let God work through your hands to bring beauty and order into their lives.
This will give your family a sense of stability and comfort,
and will make your guests feel comfortable and welcome.

Use your housekeeping time as an opportunity to give thanks
for the many blessings you have!
Be thankful for running water, a roof over your head,
hands to work with and a heart to love with!

A home with a little dust and a lot of laughter
will win the heart of God every time!

Pleasant words

sweet to the soul' and

YOU ARE SPECIAL

You are the best

You're Great

GOD LOVES YOU

I love you

You are sweet

BLESS YOU

Jesus Loves You

30

are like honey...

healthy to the body

I'm sorry

Please forgive me

I Love You

THANK YOU

31

WHAT A WONDERFUL THING TO CONSIDER THAT GOD USES YOUR LIFE
TO SPREAD THE AROMA OF HIS LOVE ♥

TO YOUR FAMILY, NEIGHBORHOOD, CHURCH . . . EVEN TO THE ENDS OF THE EARTH.

The cooking pan here represents your life,
a mixture of your knowledge, love and personal dedication to God,
stirred up with faith and heated by the fire of the Holy Spirit.
And what does this delightful aroma smell like?
It is the sweet and delicious-smelling aroma of your ordinary life
placed before God as an offering.
It is an exquisite combination of kindness, tenderheartedness, forgiveness,
righteousness, generosity, and good works!

In the Bible we are called the "salt of the earth," for as salt is a
preservative to food, so our lives and words can have a preserving
effect on the lives of others.

Sweet words are the words of life and health that we speak. Choose to
lift others up with words of kindness, truth, encouragement, hope —
even correction, seasoned with grace.

God has labeled your words of praise as the fruit of your lips, so be
willing to give away jar after jar of peachy praise to the glory of God.

The greatest witness of God's love ♥ is a life generously given to bless
the Lord and to minister to others.

Give away your life, your ♥ love, and your forgiveness . . .
for with the same measure you use to give yourself away,
blessings will be measured back to you.

We are to God the

Aroma of Christ

2 Corinthians 2:15

Love

Grace

Sweet Words

Peachy Praise

Charity Chutney

Prayer Preserves

To my Family with love

To Friends

33

By wisdom a house is
built,
and through
understanding it is
established;
through knowledge
its rooms are filled
with rare and
beautiful treasures

Proverbs 24:3,4

34

In this illustration each frame in the shadowbox represents a different aspect of being a keeper of the home. The verse is an encouragement that no matter what your age or marital status, as you grow in the wisdom, understanding, and knowledge of God you will become a woman He can use to fill a home with the rare and beautiful treasures of His love and blessings.

The teddy bear represents the gentleness and tenderness that a woman brings into the home through her loving and nurturing nature.

The sewing supplies speak of mending. As women, we are called to mend many things, from scraped knees and broken toys to broken dreams and wounded hearts.

The patchwork heart is a wonderful representation of the many personalities that make up a family and how the love of the Lord can unite them together as one.

The tools imply building in all aspects— building a house, building relationships, building character— with Jesus Christ as the foundation for all of them.

The individual hearts represent the different personalities within the family and the need each one has to be nurtured to become the unique individual God created him or her to be.

The laundry represents all the mundane chores that must be done, day after day. These elements of keeping house bring stability and a sense of order and security to all who live there.

The pie is a sweet example of being fed within the family. But, all the food we serve, whether for the body, the mind, or the spirit needs to be healthy and nourishing, causing us to grow strong and mature physically, mentally, and spiritually.

Marriage is God's design.

He looked at a man and saw he was not complete
without a suitable partner . . . so He created you.
The Lord created man and woman
to complement and complete each other.

The marriage bed speaks of the purity, beauty, and wonderful satisfaction of the physical union of husband and wife. It also symbolizes the fidelity and faithfulness of each to the other.

"His" and "Her" robes represent the two separate and unique personalities that are bound together in marriage as one.

The double wedding-ring pattern of the quilt reminds us that marital devotion and commitment are everlasting.

The Bible and devotionals are reminders that God holds your relationship in the palm of His hand. And you hold it in your prayers. Pray for one another. Pray together, read together, and rejoice together.

The tray signifies the communion of husband and wife. It speaks not only of the physical union but of having all things in common, of sharing material blessings as well as the blessings and burdens of life and love itself.

The candle reminds us of the light of Christ, which should always be lit to give focus and direction to every aspect of your marriage.

The two shall become one

Genesis 2:24

What is Love?

Love is patient

Love is kind

Love does not envy

Love does not boast

Love is not rude

Love is not proud

Love always protects

Love always trusts

Love always hopes

1 Corinthians 13:4-7

39

If you're like most of us, you've found yourself, more than once, searching frantically in the closet and declaring you have nothing at all to wear! What you see either doesn't fit, is not appropriate for the occasion, or needs to be laundered!

Just as you would never think of wearing dirty clothes or even hanging them in your closet, God calls you as His child to take off the dirty rags you've been wearing — old attitudes and bad habits — and put on the clean clothing of godly attitudes and habits that He wants to develop in your life.

God has filled your spiritual closet with the most beautiful and well-made wardrobe you could ever imagine! He created these garments Himself. They are guaranteed to fit well and to last long.

Open your closet and see:
the garment of praise for the spirit of heaviness,
the undergarments of tender mercies, humility, and forgiveness,
the belt of truth, the vest of right living,
well-fitting shoes of the Good News of peace,
the protective head-covering of salvation
and much more!

♥ Most importantly... put on love! ♥

As you learn to dress from your spiritual closet you will be able to teach your children and others how to do the same.

Above all these things put on love

Colossians 3:14

41

Create in me a clean heart O God

Psalm 51:10

42

We live in a culture that is consumed with cleanliness. We have an overwhelming need to be clean, but all the detergents in the world cannot clean the impurities of the heart.

God calls these impurities sin. When you accept Jesus Christ as your Savior, your sins are forgiven and you are washed white as snow. You may continue to "scrub" your outside clean in order to gain God's approval, but Jesus shed His blood on the cross, once and for all, in order to cleanse your guilt and shame and make you acceptable before a holy God.

When you look sincerely into the Word of God
you will learn how your life
can reflect more and more
the character and the glory of God.
This is the reflection that you want to be mirrored
in the lives of your children as well.

God has wrapped you in His own divine
robe of righteousness — there is none so beautiful!

As you allow God to soothe your wounds with His balm
of healing, turn your sadness into joy,
and fill your heart with His love,
you will find yourself better able to minister
to the needs of those you love —
to comfort them with the comfort that you have received.

43

A merry heart does

Tablets of Gladness

Pills of Praise

Love

good like a medicine.

OIL
of
JOY

Proverbs 17:22

How appropriate that a dressing table with a large mirror should be called a "vanity." It beckons us to come, sit a spell, and find a sense of satisfaction, perhaps even a bit of pride, in our reflection. But God is pleased when you look in the mirror and find an inner peace and contentment, knowing that He created your features and, in fact, has numbered each hair on your head.

Don't spend your time worrying about your outward appearance —
how you style your hair, the jewelry you wear,
the cost of your perfume or the name brand of your clothes —
rather, let your beauty shine forth from within.
Let the hidden person of your heart
reflect a gentle and quiet spirit,
This is precious in the sight of God.

Your value is not determined by your outward beauty.
It is based on the truth of who God says you are:
His dearly beloved child, formed in His image,
created with a purpose and a calling.

As a godly woman and a representative of Jesus Christ
a clean and attractive appearance is an important example
to your children and to the world,
but more important is the care and nurture of a kind and loving heart.

I am fearfully and wonderfully made.

Psalm 139:14

Encourage
each other
and
build each
other up.

1 Thessalonians 5:11

You are a vessel designed to pour out
God's love and encouragement to those around you.

He says your words hold the power of life and death.
Through words alone you can bless and build up or wound and destroy.

The world is full of hurting people.
Make it a daily habit to pour out life, building others up
and strengthening them through positive and encouraging words.

There is no greater need for encouraging others
than in your own home.
Your husband and your children need to know
how much you love them and how special they really are!

Ask God to show you practical ways to express His love to others today.
It might be a vase of flowers or a quiet embrace.
It might be a phone call filled with bright and cheery words of hope
or it might be a note of gentle encouragement.
Whether your note is penned on beautiful stationery
or on a sticky note in a child's lunchbox,
you are the scented ink God uses
to spread the fragrance of Christ's love.

What have you done (or would like to do) to reach out to others?

In the center of this desk just
as it needs to be in the center of your
life, is the Bible , God's written Word.
His Word illumines your way, as a lamp gives light to
your feet when you walk the rough and rocky path of life.

The cup represents the refreshing and rest that is available
as you keep God's promises in your heart as encouragement.

The bottle of oil depicts the anointing of the Holy Spirit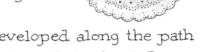

The apple is a picture of the fruit that is developed along the path
of your life as you grow in the truth and knowledge of the Lord Jesus.

The plainly wrapped gift illustrates the fact that Jesus gave up His
glory and humbled Himself as a man to give you the greatest gift of all,
eternal life.

The books are a reminder to study God's Word diligently.

Just as this illustration is surrounded with the written word
and a border of hearts, so may your whole life be
encompassed with the truth and guidance of the
Word of God and the love of Jesus
Christ.

Your word is a lamp to my feet

and a light to my path.

Be hospitable to one another. . .

1 Peter 4:9

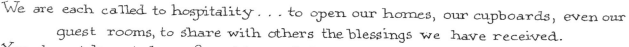

Be hospitable to one another . . . without grumbling.

We are each called to hospitality . . . to open our homes, our cupboards, even our guest rooms, to share with others the blessings we have received.

You do not have to have fine china and the budget to serve steak, but you do need to offer the gifts God has given you to serve and bless others.

The Lord loves a cheerful giver, so give yourself away generously and joyfully to others . . . your time, your compassion, your open door.

The guest room suggests a pleasant refuge, a place of acceptance, comfort, and love. ♥

The gift of love on the bed is our gift to the Lord in giving ourselves to others. ♥

The cup of tea represents a time of refreshing and rest.

The heart cookies remind us that as we are hospitable to others, they will "taste" and see that the Lord is good. ♥

The flowers suggest the reflection of Christ's beauty through a generous heart. ♥

The books remind us to share not only our lives but the Good News of new life in Christ.

The lamp symbolizes that Jesus is the light of the world.

The clock reminds us to make the most of every opportunity to reach out to others in love.

Remember to welcome strangers,
you just might welcome an angel.

Guests we have entertained in our home.

Children are a gift from God!

They are tiny packages filled with tremendous potential,
given to bring great blessing —
as well as a challenge here and there!
God gives them to us, not to be possessed or controlled,
but to be loved and nurtured.

Each little bundle is created with the greatest care
in the mother's womb, woven carefully in God's own image.
No two children are exactly alike.
Each child has a distinct and unique personality with
strengths and weaknesses, gifts and abilities, desires and dreams
to be nurtured and molded with love, discipline, and instruction.
God has a perfect plan for each child's life . . .
a future with purpose and hope.

Just as proper nutrition is needed for children to develop
strong and healthy bodies,
the pure milk of God's Word is vital to nourish
the heart and character of every child.
And God uses a parent's love not only to teach and instruct
but also to wrap a child's heart
with the warmth of comfort, protection, and blessing.

Children are
a heritage
from
the Lord.

Psalm 127:3

.. His
children,
the sheep
of His pasture.

Psalm 100:3

Imitate me,

Do not provoke your children
to anger, but bring them up in
the discipline and instruction of
the Lord.

Ephesians 6:4

The joy of
the Lord
is my
strength.

Nehemiah 8:10

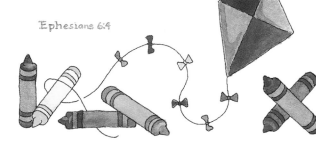

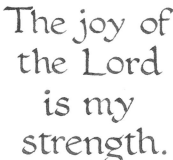

60

Train up a child in the way he should go and when he is old he will not depart from it.

Proverbs 22:6

as I imitate Christ

I Corinthians 11:1

For the moment all discipline seems painful rather than pleasant, later it yields the peaceful fruit of righteousness to those who have been trained by it. Hebrews 12:11

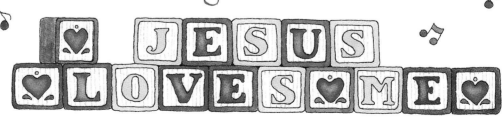

JESUS LOVES ME

Aa Bb Cc Dd Ee
Ff Gg Hh Ii Jj
Wisdom
is better
than
wealth

Learning begins at birth!
What skills are your children learning?
Are you able to identify any gifts or talents
that God has given them?
Record those things here...

Notes

62

My Children, My Delight

Being a teenager today is not easy. The world woos, tugs, and pulls from every direction. Yet God's desire for our young people is that no one would have opportunity to despise or criticize them, but would respect them because of their godly lifestyles. He calls our teens to be an example, not only to their peers but to the whole church, by their words, their faith, and their conduct.

That's a tall order!

A good question might be . . . who are their examples?

Ultimately, the greatest example is Jesus Himself,
but teens also need to see the reality of Christ in the lives of their parents.

No one has more influence.

Be a godly example and a source of strength for your teens (or any young person you know):

Love them unconditionally.

Encourage them not to neglect but to exercise the gifts God has given them.

Be their loudest cheerleader! Cheer them on in the race they're running both in the Lord and in their daily lives.

Reward them by letting them know they are #1 in you book, no matter what.

Teach them God's truths in practical ways (without preaching).

Prepare them to stand on their own, and prepare yourself to eventually let them go — and trust God.

Let
no one
despise your
youth.

Love

1 Timothy 4:12

Your
Word
I have
hidden
in my heart...

. . . that I might not
sin against You.

Psalm 119:11

Behold,
how good
and
how pleasant
it is

Psalm 133:1

. . . for families to live together in harmony

The family room is the focal point of the home,
the gathering place where all are welcome. Here lives are shared
and memories are made. This is the room known for its warmth,
filled to overflowing with love, joy, and laughter.
Whether playing games, singing songs,
reading stories, or watching videos,
this is where the family gathers and friends are welcome.

This is also the room that invites a party! Birthdays. Anniversaries.
Holidays.   A lost tooth or a new found friend!
Find reasons to celebrate! Turn the ordinary into extra-ordinary!

♥

Although a hearth is inviting, the true warmth of a home is
created with open arms and loving kindness.

♥

Make time to enjoy old family traditions and even create some new ones.
The memories you establish now
will refresh the hearts of future generations.
Let their hearts recall times of reflecting on God's goodness,
reading Bible stories, singing praises, and sharing together in the joy of
the Lord.

Even though you may have a great devotional time
with the Lord in the morning, it can be easy to "forget" Him
as you are challenged throughout the day with children,
chores, and everyday cares.

But just as you cherish and display old photos  and
memorabelia around the house to remind you
of important people and special events, why not hang Scripture
on your walls to remind you what a great God you serve —
to remind you what He has done for you,
and what He has promised for your future.

Be encouraged to place God's
words of encouragement and direction
first in your heart and then prominently in your home —
on wall plaques , refrigerator magnets,
even scribbled scraps of paper taped to the bathroom mirror,
This will demonstrate to your children how much you value
God's Word and will be a tool to teach them as well.

Let us not "forget" the Lord!

You shall love
the Lord your God
with all your heart,
with all your soul,
and
with all your strength.

Deuteronomy 6:5

Your soul
shall be like
a well
watered
garden.

The Lord
is my
Shepherd

71

You are His workmanship

New Creation

Ephesians 2:10

When you take time to smell the roses,
gaze at the stars, or delight in the colors of fall leaves,
you will find that the Creator of the universe made no two alike.
The same is true of His children. Each one is special,
as distinctive as the bolts of fabric on the shelf.

God made you one of a kind!
He knit you together in your mother's womb.
There is no one on the face of this earth like you.
No one else has your unique combination of personality,
gifts and talents, strengths and life experiences.
There is a path before you that you alone can walk.
There is a purpose that you alone can fulfill.

When you begin to accept and embrace this truth about yourself,
it will truly set you free. When you learn to accept yourself as God's design,
you will also be more willing to accept your husband, your children,
and others around you as the people God created them to be.

Ask God to give you the desire and the wisdom to accept and nurture
each person's individuality, including your own.
Help those you love to be all that God designed them to be
instead of trying to mold them into someone they are not —
into someone you think they should be.

Remember that God has the perfect plan for their lives as well as for your own.

74

A day
hemmed
♡
in prayer
seldom
unravels

The attic is a place for hiding things. Perhaps in your house it's the basement, or a closet. You hide things there that you don't want others to see; things that once had value but now seem outdated, broken or useless.

Do you ever feel broken? Outdated? Of little value?
Tossed in a corner like an old worn out quilt?

In a sense, you are like a quilt, pieced together with the fabric of your personality, your experiences, and your choices. When you first come to God, your quilt may not be very pretty. It may show wear from being tossed around and neglected. It may bear the stains of rejection and the marks of a broken heart. Torn by unfulfilled dreams and broken relationships, soiled by bad habits and poor choices, you may find it difficult to believe that God truly loves you and has a special plan for your life. But He does!

You are not hidden from God's eyes. He sees you and wants to hold the quilt of your life close to His heart. He knows the story of your quilt and wants to wash away every stain and blemish with His mercy and grace. He will not take away the old, worn places for they are part of your character. Instead He will touch them with new life through Christ and restitch the pieces of your quilt together with the beautiful threads of love and compassion.

You are God's workmanship, a quilt of beauty to behold.
He wants to use you to bring glory to His name,
to wrap a blessing around others who need your love.

He restores
my soul

Psalm 23:3

Behold I stand
at the door and knock

Revelation 3:20